# Human Body Activity Book
## For kids in Grades 4-6

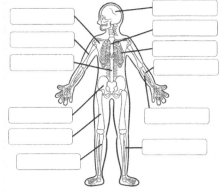

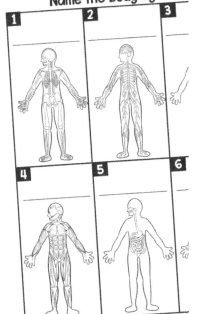

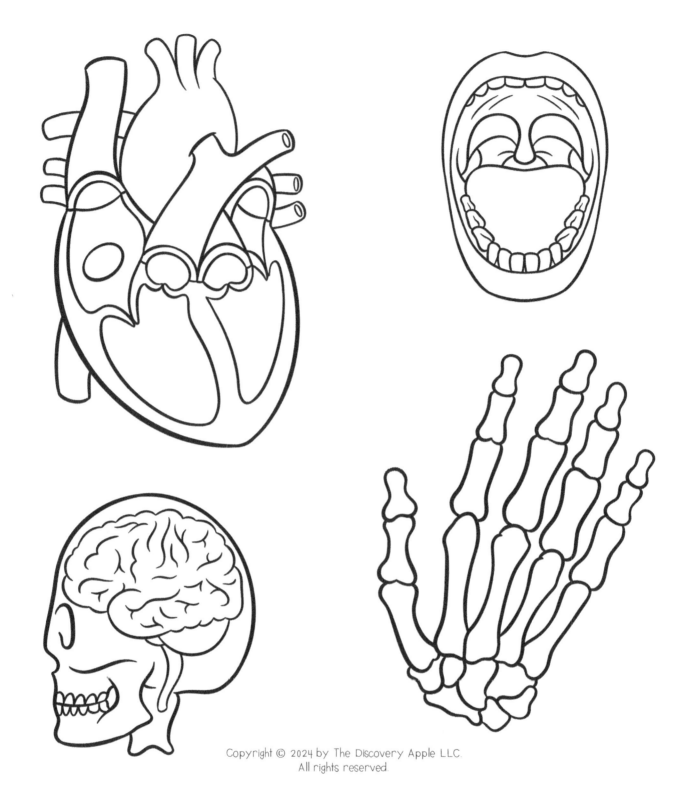

Written by Fatema Ghazi
Illustrations by Mariam Ghazi

Contact the author:
Fatema@thediscoveryapple.com

# This book belongs to:

_____

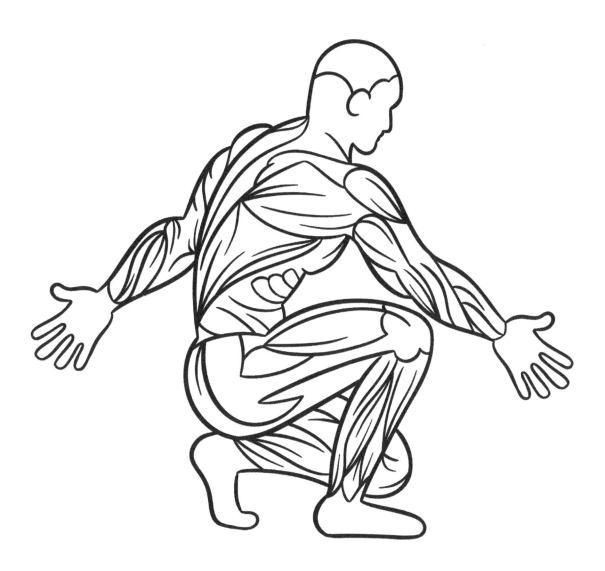

# Table of Contents

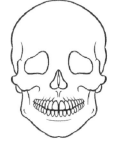

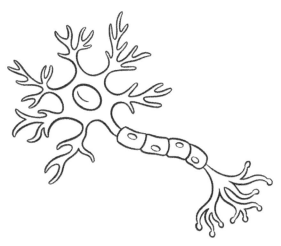

# The Respiratory System

# Exploring The Respiratory System

Your lungs are a big part of the respiratory system that allows you to breathe. Other parts of the respiratory system include the nose, mouth, throat, voice box, and windpipe. The respiratory system's main job is to bring oxygen into our bodies and send carbon dioxide, a waste gas, out. Every cell in your body needs oxygen in order to live.

When oxygen gets in the lungs, the oxygen is moved into the bloodstream and carried through your body. Oxygen is exchanged for carbon dioxide in your bloodstream, which is then removed and exhaled as a part of the breathing process. This entire process, called gas exchange, is automatically performed by your lungs and respiratory system.

Your lungs are pink and squishy that take up most of the space in your chest. You have two lungs that are not the same size. Your left lung is a bit smaller than your right lung. This extra space on the left leaves room for your heart. Your rib cage protects your lungs. Your rib cage is made up of 12 sets of ribs. Beneath the lungs is the diaphragm. Your diaphragm is a muscle that works with your lungs to allow you to breathe in (inhale) and breathe out (exhale).

When you breathe out, the air moves up the trachea and flows past the vocal cords. The vocal cords start to vibrate back and forth caused by the moving air. As they vibrate, they make the sound people hear when you speak or sing, also known as your voice.

Coughing and sneezing is also performed by your respiratory system. Did you know that when you cough or sneeze, your actually protecting your body from harmful substances? It is a way of forcing the substances your body does not need or want out of your body.

Do you know why you yawn? It means your brain detected low oxygen levels in the lungs, triggering the yawning. Yawning helps bring in a large amount of oxygen.

# Exploring The Respiratory System

After reading the passage, answer the questions below.

1. Which of the following is <u>not</u> a part of the respiratory system?

   a) Lungs
   b) Nose
   c) Heart
   d) Voice box

2. What is the main job of the respiratory system?

   _____

   _____

3. Where does oxygen get carried throughout your body?

   _____

4. What is removed from the bloodstream and then gets exhaled?

   _____

5. Why is your left lung a bit smaller than your right lung?

   _____

   _____

6. What protects your lungs?

   _____

   _____

7. What is the muscle that works with your lungs to allow you to inhale and exhale?

   _____

8. What vibrates and causes the sound people hear when you talk?

   _____

9. What happens when you cough or sneeze?

   _____

   _____

10. When your brain detects low oxygen levels in the lungs, it triggers you to

   _____

# Respiratory System
## Vocabulary

**Lungs:** 2 bag-like organs located in the chest that allow you to take in oxygen and release carbon dioxide

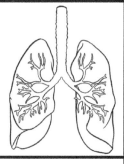

**Respiration:** the act of breathing in and breathing out

**Inhale:** taking in oxygen

**Larynx:** also known as your voice box where air passes through on its way to the lungs and produces vocal sounds

**Exhale:** giving off carbon dioxide

**Trachea:** also known as your windpipe that carries air to and from the lungs

**Nasal Cavity:** the inside of your nose where air passes through

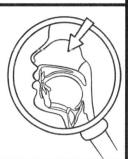

**Cilia:** Tiny hair-like structures that protect the nasal passageways and other parts of the respiratory tract. They filter out dust and other particles that enter the nose when we breathe air.

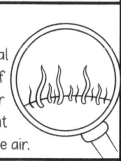

**Alveoli:** tiny air sacs in the lungs where the exchange of oxygen and carbon dioxide takes place

**Diaphragm:** A large dome-shaped muscle located below the lungs that helps you to breathe in and breathe out.

# The Respiratory System

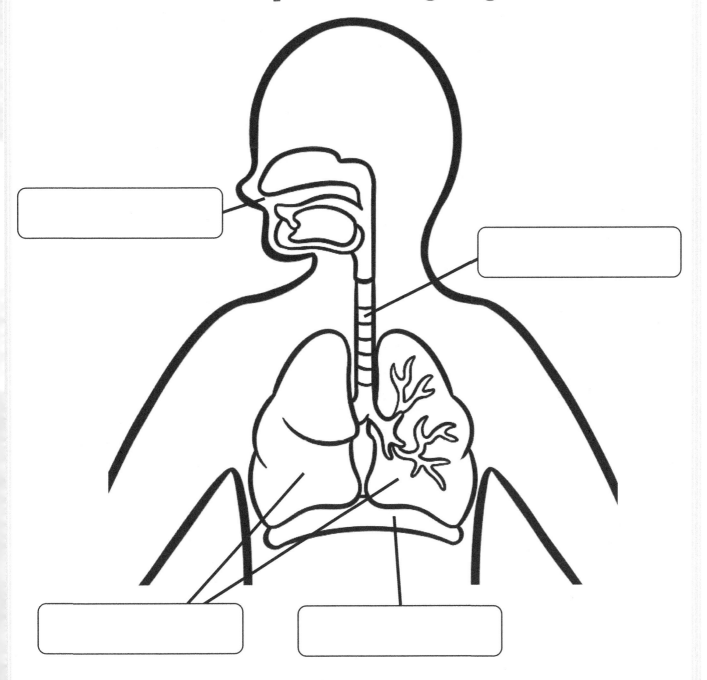

## Word Bank

| Lungs | Trachea |
|---|---|
| Nasal Cavity | Diaphragm |

# VOCAB MATCH

Find the definition for each word. Write the correct letter under each word.

| | |
|---|---|
| **1.** Lungs | **2.** Inhale |
| **3.** Exhale | **4.** Nasal Cavity |
| **5.** Alveoli | **6.** Respiration |
| **7.** Larynx | **8.** Trachea |
| **9.** Cilia | **10.** Diaphragm |

**A** also known as your windpipe that carries air to and from the lungs

**B** taking in oxygen

**C** A large dome-shaped muscle located below the lungs that helps you to breathe in and breathe out

**D** tiny air sacs in the lungs where the exchange of oxygen and carbon dioxide takes place

**E** the inside of your nose where air passes through

**F** 2 bag-like organs located in the chest that allow you to take in oxygen and release carbon dioxide

**G** also known as your voice box where air passes through on its way to the lungs and produces vocal sounds

**H** Tiny hair-like structures that protect the nasal passageways and other parts of the respiratory tract by filtering out dust and other particles that enter the nose

**I** giving off carbon dioxide

**J** the act of breathing in and breathing out

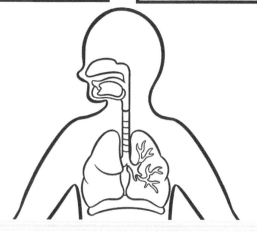

12

# The Digestive System

The length of our digestive system is around 20 – 30 feet.
20 feet is about the same height of a giraffe!

# A Journey Through the Digestive System

Did you know that what you ate for breakfast today is being broken down into substances that your organs and cells in your body can use? That is the job of your digestive system. Your body needs food to provide it with energy, vitamins, and minerals. Depending on what you ate, it could take your food around 24 hours to travel through the digestive system, which is 20 to 30 feet long!

There are several stages of the digestive system, and it all starts with the mouth. Once you put something in your mouth, your strong teeth start to chomp your food, breaking them down into smaller pieces. Your tongue will then squeeze the chewed food into lumps you can swallow, pushing them back towards your throat. Your saliva moistens the food, making it easier to swallow. Your saliva is also full of chemicals, called enzymes, that help break down the food.

The next stage on our journey through the digestive system is the stomach. Did you know that your stomach is about the size of a tennis ball when it is empty and stretches to the size of a football when it is filled with food? Your food will hang around in your stomach for about 4 hours. Your stomach releases juices and acid that break down the food even more and kills a lot of harmful bacteria so that you don't get sick.

Once the food in your stomach turn very watery, kind of like soup, it is ready to be squirted into your small intestine. Your small intestine is not really that small. If you stretch out an adult's small intestine, it would measure about 22 feet long! The first part of the small intestine works with the juices from the pancreas and liver to break down our food even more. The second part is where your food gets absorbed from the small intestine and into our body through the blood.

The last stop on this digestive journey is the large intestine. The large intestine is fatter than the small intestine, but if you spread it out, it would measure only about 5 feet long. Any food that the body does not need or can't use is sent here and then later leaves the body as waste.

# A Journey Through the Digestive System

After reading the passage, answer the questions below.

1. Which of the following is a function of the digestive system?

    a) delivers oxygen to all parts of the body
    b) breaks down food into small substances your body can use
    c) protects the body's soft organs
    d) controls your breathing and thinking

2. Why does your body need food?

   _____

   _____

3. Explain the very first stage of the digestive system.

   _____

   _____

   _____

4. Why is it a good thing to have saliva?

   _____

   _____

   _____

5. For how long does your food hang around in your stomach?

   _____

6. What is the function of your stomach?

   _____

   _____

7. True or False: If stretched out, your small intestine is shorter than your large intestine.

   _____

8. Your food gets absorbed from the _____ and into our body

   through the _____.

9. Explain the last stage of the digestive system.

   _____

   _____

# Digestive System
## Vocabulary

**Digestion:** the process of breaking down food into smaller parts so that your body can use them

**Small Intestine:** an organ that breaks down food from the stomach and absorbs most of the nutrients from the food

**Enzymes:** these are special types of proteins that help break down, digest, and absorb food

**Large Intestine:** any food that the body doesn't need or cant use is sent to this organ and later leaves the body as waste

**Pancreas:** a long tube shaped organ that produces enzymes and help control glucose (sugar) levels

**Stomach:** an organ located on the left side of the upper abdomen that stores, mixes, and mashes food

**Glucose:** comes from the food we eat and is the main type of sugar in the blood that provides energy for your cells

**Pharynx:** also called the throat; helps with eating and breathing

**Bile:** a yellowish- green fluid produced by the liver that helps the body absorb fat into the bloodstream

**Esophagus:** It is like a stretchy tube that moves food from the back of the throat to the stomach

# The Digestive System

[blank label boxes positioned around a diagram of the digestive system]

## Word Bank

| Rectum | Esophagus | Small Intestine |
|---|---|---|
| Stomach | Mouth | Large Intestine |
| Liver | Pancreas | |

# VOCAB MATCH

Find the definition for each word. Write the correct letter under each word.

| 1. Digestion | 2. Stomach |
| --- | --- |
| _____ | _____ |

| 3. Small Intestine | 4. Large Intestine |
| --- | --- |
| _____ | _____ |

| 5. Pharynx | 6. Bile |
| --- | --- |
| _____ | _____ |

| 7. Glucose | 8. Esophagus |
| --- | --- |
| _____ | _____ |

| 9. Pancreas | 10. Enzymes |
| --- | --- |
| _____ | _____ |

**A** also called the throat; helps with eating and breathing

**B** It is like a stretchy tube that moves food from the back of the throat to the stomach

**C** the process of breaking down food into smaller parts so that your body can use them

**D** an organ that breaks down food from the stomach and absorbs most of the nutrients from the food

**E** these are special types of proteins that help break down, digest, and absorb food

**F** a yellowish-green fluid produced by the liver that helps the body absorb fat into the bloodstream.

**G** any food that the body doesn't need or cant use is sent to this organ and later leaves the body as waste

**H** an organ located on the left side of the upper abdomen that stores, mixes, and mashes food

**I** comes from the food we eat and is the main type of sugar in the blood that provides energy for your cells

**J** a long tube shaped organ that produces enzymes and help control glucose (sugar) levels

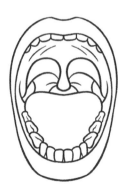
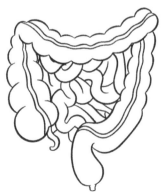
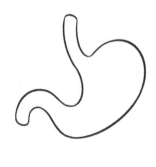

# The Nervous System

# The Control of the Nervous System

The nervous system controls everything you do, including how you think, feel, learn, walk, and talk. It also controls things you are less aware of, such as the beating of your heart. The nervous system is made up of your brain, spinal cord, and all the nerves of your body.

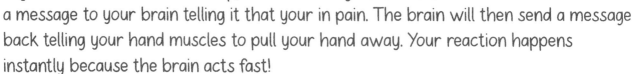

Your brain is the control center that sends and receives information about what is happening in the body and around it. It basically controls all the body's functions. When the brain receives a message from somewhere in your body, your brain will tell the body how to react. For example, if you touch a hot bowl of soup, the nerves in your skin send a message to your brain telling it that your in pain. The brain will then send a message back telling your hand muscles to pull your hand away. Your reaction happens instantly because the brain acts fast!

Your spinal cord is like a major highway to and from the brain. This is where the messages are being sent back and forth. The spinal cord contains billions of nerve cells, or neurons, which join together to make nerves. The nerves branch out to every organ and body part.

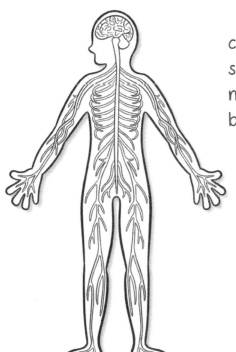

The nervous system is divided in two parts: the central nervous system and the peripheral nervous system. The brain and the spinal cord make up the central nervous system. The nerves that go through the entire body make up the peripheral nervous system.

Your brain and spinal cord are protected by bone. The brain is protected inside the skull and the spinal cord is protected by a set of ring-shaped bones called vertebrae.

# The Control of The Nervous System

After reading the passage, answer the questions below.

1. Which of the following is a function of the nervous system?

    a) protects your organs
    b) breaks down food into small molecules
    c) controls the way you think and feel
    d) removes waste

2. What is the nervous system made up of?

    _____

    _____

3. What does your brain control?

    _____

4. What is responsible in sending messages to your brain when you feel pain?

    _____

5. Messages are sent back and forth along your _____.

6. What is your central nervous system made up of?

    _____

    _____

7. What is your peripheral nervous system made up of?

    _____

8. What protects your brain?

    _____

9. What protects your spinal cord?

    _____

# Nervous System
## Vocabulary

**Brain:** a complex organ that controls all of the body's functions such as thought, memory, emotion, touch, vision, breathing, and hunger

**Spinal Cord:** a thin bundle of nerves that is like a major highway to and from the brain.

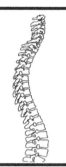

**Nerves:** strings of neurons that send messages or signals to and from the brain

**Cerebellum:** located at the back of the brain that controls balance, movement, and coordination

**Central Nervous System:** consists of the brain and spinal cord

**Cerebrum:** the biggest part of the brain that is the thinking part of the brain and controls your voluntary muscles

**Peripheral Nervous System:** consists of the nerves that go through the whole body

**Brain Stem:** Located at the base of the brain beneath the cerebrum. It is in charge of all the functions your body needs to stay alive, such as breathing, digesting food, and circulating blood

**Impulses:** an electrical signal carried by nerve cells when stimulated; also known as "action potential"

**Reflex:** An automatic, or involuntary, action that your body does in response to something without thinking about it

# The Nervous System

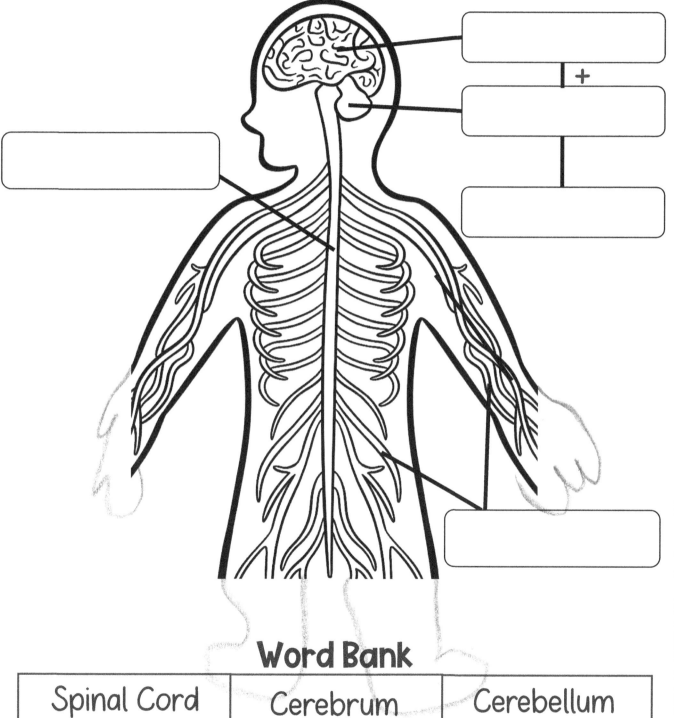

+

## Word Bank

| Spinal Cord | Cerebrum | Cerebellum |
|---|---|---|
| | Brain | Nerves |

# VOCAB MATCH

Find the definition for each word. Write the correct letter under each word.

| 1. Brain | 2. Nerves |
|---|---|
| _____ | _____ |
| 3. Central Nervous System | 4. Peripheral Nervous System |
| _____ | _____ |
| 5. Impulses | 6. Spinal Cord |
| _____ | _____ |
| 7. Cerebellum | 8. Cerebrum |
| _____ | _____ |
| 9. Brain Stem | 10. Reflex |
| _____ | _____ |

**A** a thin bundle of nerves that is like a major highway to and from the brain

**B** taking in oxygen

**C** the biggest part of the brain that is the thinking part of the brain and controls your voluntary muscles

**D** strings of neurons that send messages or signals to and from the brain

**E** an electrical signal carried by nerve cells when stimulated; also known as "action potential"

**F** located at the back of the brain that controls balance, movement, and coordination

**G** consists of the nerves that go through the whole body

**H** a complex organ that controls all of the body's functions such as thought, memory, emotion, touch, vision, breathing, and hunger.

**I** Located at the base of the brain beneath the cerebrum that is in charge of all the functions your body needs to stay alive such as breathing, digesting food, and circulating blood

**J** consists of the brain and spinal cord

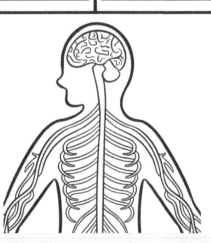

# The Skeletal System

When a baby is born, the skeleton is made up of around 300 bones. When they grow up into adults, they end up with 206 bones because some bones have fused together.

# Understanding the Skeletal System

The skeletal system is made up of all the bones, tendons, ligaments, and cartilage in the human body. There are 206 bones in the skeletal system and they all play very important roles. Some bones support us, some protect us, and others allow us to move around by supporting our muscles.

There are three main layers of a bone. The outermost part of the bone is smooth and hard, and it protects its interior. This is called the compact bone. Then there is the spongy layer which is the soft flexible part of the bone called the spongy bone. The innermost part of the bone is made of a jellylike material called bone marrow.

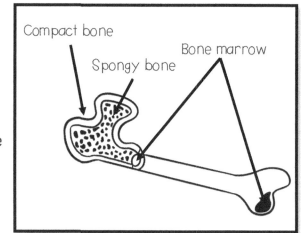

There are two kinds of bone marrow: yellow and red. Red bone marrow is where blood cells are produced. Fat cells usually make up yellow bone marrow.

All of the bones in the body come together in a very unique way. The places where these bones meet and connect are called joints. There are four main types of movable joints: ball and socket, hinge, pivot, and gliding.

The ball and socket joint allows you to move most freely because of the way it's connected. A good example of this type of joint is your hips and shoulders. Your elbow is an example of a hinge joint because it only moves back and forth in one direction. A pivot joint allows for a twisting and rotating movement, so that you can keep your head bobbing to all your favorite songs. Last but not least the gliding joint. This type of joint can be fount in your palms. It lets your bones glide past one another on the flat part of the bone.

At the ends of the bones you will find a tough flexible material called cartilage. Cartilage allows the bones to rub smoothly against each other. That is how bones are connected to each other, but what connects our bones to our muscles? Tendons are what keep our bones and muscles connected which allows us to move around however we like.

# Understanding the Skeletal System

After reading the passage, answer the questions below.

1. Which of the following is <u>not</u> a function of the skeletal system?

    a) supports our bodies
    b) protects our internal organs
    c) delivers oxygen to all parts of the body
    d) allows us to move around

2. The skeletal system is made up of all the _____,

    _____, _____, and

    _____ in the human body.

3. How many bones are in the skeletal system?

    _____

4. What are the three main layers of a bone?

    _____

5. The smooth outer layer of the bone is called the _____.

6. What is the innermost jellylike part of the bone called?

    a) spongy bone
    b) bone marrow
    c) compact bone
    d) jelly bone

7. What are the two types of bone marrow?

    _____

8. What are the places where bones meet and connect called?

    _____

# Understanding the Skeletal System

After reading the passage, answer the questions below.

9. Which joint allows you to move the most freely?

       a) hinge joint
       b) ball and socket joint
       c) gliding joint
       d) pivot joint

10. Give an example of a hinge joint.

_____

11. A pivot joint allows for a _____ and

_____ movement.

12. What type of joint can be found in your palms?

       a) hinge joint
       b) ball and socket joint
       c) gliding joint
       d) pivot joint

13. True or false: Cartilage allows the bones to rub smoothly against each   other.

       a) True
       b) False

14. What connects our bones to our muscles?

_____

# Skeletal System
## Vocabulary

**Skeleton:** made up of many bones that create a structure for our body, allows you to move, and protects your internal organs

**Ribs:** curved bones that form the skeletal structure of the chest wall and protects your body's lungs and heart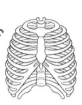

**Joints:** the place where two bones meet.
Example: Your knees and elbows

**Pelvis:** bowl shaped structure that supports the spine

**Ligament:** tough bands of tissue which attaches bone to bone

**Skull:** a bone structure that forms the head and face and protects the brain

**Cartilage:** firm, rubbery tissue that cushions bones at joints.
Example: the tip of your nose, the top of your ear

**Calcium:** a mineral that is stored in your bones and teeth to keep them strong

**Bone Marrow:** a spongy substance found inside your bones that produce blood cells

**Tibia:** the inner and larger of the two bones in the lower leg, between the knees and ankle

# The Skeletal System

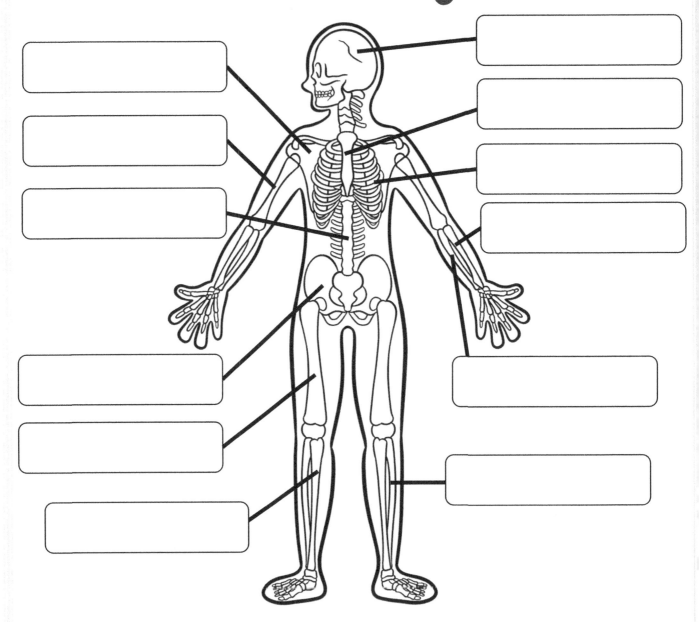

## Word Bank

| Fibula | Radius | Humerus | Pelvis |
|--------|--------|---------|--------|
| Skull | Ribs | Tibia | Ulna |
| Scapula | Femur | Spine | Sternum |

# VOCAB MATCH

Find the definition for each word. Write the correct letter under each word.

| | |
|---|---|
| **1.** Skeleton | **2.** Joints |
| **3.** Ligament | **4.** Cartilage |
| **5.** Bone Marrow | **6.** Ribs |
| **7.** Pelvis | **8.** Skull |
| **9.** Calcium | **10.** Tibia |

**A** a bone structure that forms the head and face and protects the brain

**B** firm, rubbery tissue that cushions bones at joints. Example: the tip of your nose, the top of your ear

**C** a spongy substance found inside your bones that produce blood cells

**D** the inner and larger of the two bones in the lower leg, between the knees and ankle

**E** made up of many bones that create a structure for our body, allows you to move, and protects your internal organs

**F** bowl shaped structure that supports the spine

**G** the place where two bones meet. Example: Your knees and elbows

**H** tough bands of tissue which attaches bone to bone

**I** curved bones that form the skeletal structure of the chest wall and protects your body's lungs and heart

**J** a mineral that is stored in your bones and teeth to keep them strong

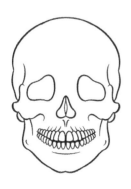  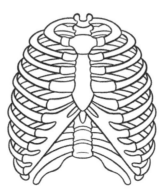 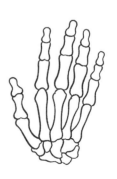

# The Muscular System

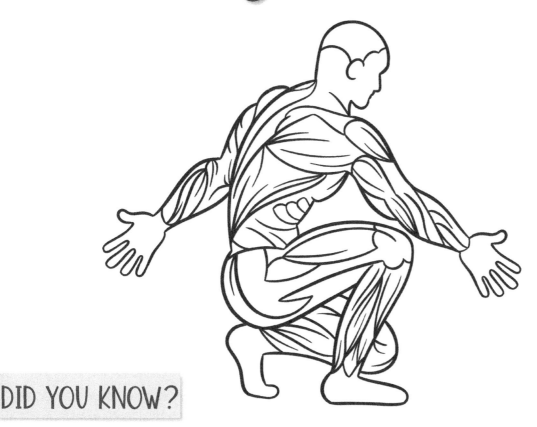

# The Powerful Muscular System

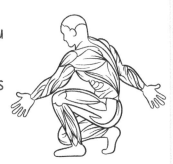

Your muscles are what help your body move and function, whether it's wiggling your fingers or jumping up and down. "Did you know that you have over 600 muscles? That's right! It's not only the muscles you show when you flex your arm. Each muscle has its own special job, such as protecting your skeleton and internal organs, keeping you warm when it's cold, cooling you down when you're hot, and helping you digest your food.

You have muscles that you can control, like the ones in your arms and legs, called **voluntary** muscles, and muscles that you can't control, like your heart, called **involuntary** muscles. Your heart is one powerful muscle that beats 4000 beats in one hour!

You have three different types of muscles in your body: smooth muscle, cardiac muscle, and skeletal muscle. **Smooth muscles** are involuntary muscles because you can't control this type of muscle. They basically work without us having to think about them. These muscles do not connect to your bones, but they control the organs within your body. For example, in your stomach, your smooth muscles tighten up and relax to allow food to travel through the body. You can also find smooth muscles in your bladder. When these muscles are relaxed, they allow you to hold your pee until you reach the bathroom. Then, your smooth muscles contract so that you can push the pee out.

**Skeletal muscles** are the muscles you use to move around. These muscles are attached to your bones and they pull on them to make movement. These are the only voluntary muscles because you can control them with signals from your brain. Skeletal

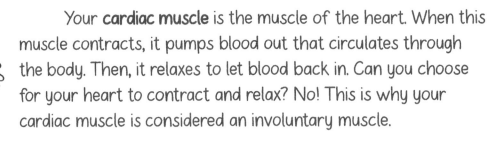

muscles move your arms, legs, and your jaw up and down so that you can chew your food.

Your **cardiac muscle** is the muscle of the heart. When this muscle contracts, it pumps blood out that circulates through the body. Then, it relaxes to let blood back in. Can you choose for your heart to contract and relax? No! This is why your cardiac muscle is considered an involuntary muscle.

# The Powerful Muscular System

After reading the passage, answer the questions below.

1.  Which of the following is <u>not</u> a function of the muscular system?

    a) protects your organs
    b) helps you digest your food
    c) pumps our heart and blood through our body
    d) controls your thoughts

2.  How many muscles do you have in your body?

    _____

3.  Muscles you can control are called _____ and muscles

    you can't control are called _____ .

4.  Which of the following is considered a voluntary muscle?

    a)  Smooth Muscle
    b)  Skeletal Muscle
    c)  Cardiac Muscle
    d)  Involuntary Muscle

5.  Which type of muscle controls the organs in your body such as your bladder?

    _____

6.  Why is your cardiac muscle considered involuntary?

    _____

    _____

7.  Which type of muscle helps you raise your hand?

    _____

# Muscular System
## Vocabulary

**Muscular System:** made up of all of our muscles together and is responsible for the movement of the human body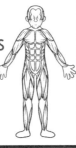

**Skeletal Muscles:** voluntary muscles that are attached to your bones and create movement

**Muscles:** an organ made up of cells called fiber tissue that can relax and contract to allow movement

**Cardiac Muscle:** involuntary muscle found only in the heart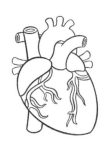

**Voluntary Muscles:** the muscles that you can control

**Striated:** a fancy word that means striped; your skeletal muscles are sometimes called striated because the light and dark parts of the muscle fibers make them look striped

**Involuntary Muscles:** the muscles you can't control such as your heart

**Muscles Contraction:** when a muscle becomes thicker and shorter

**Smooth Muscles:** involuntary muscles that control the organs within your body. Example: In your stomach, smooth muscles tighten up and relax to allow food to travel through the body.

**Tendon:** a tough band of tissue that connects muscles to bones

# The Muscular System

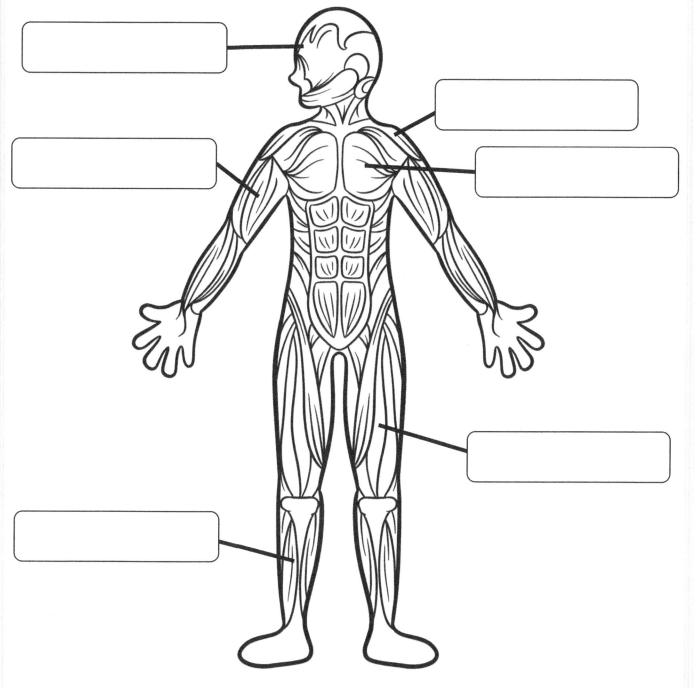

## Word Bank

| Frontalis | Biceps | Pectoralis |
|---|---|---|
| Quadriceps | Tibialis anterior | Deltoid |

# VOCAB MATCH

Find the definition for each word. Write the correct letter under each word.

| | |
|---|---|
| **1.** Muscular System | **2.** Muscle |
| **3.** Voluntary Muscles | **4.** Involuntary Muscles |
| **5.** Smooth muscles | **6.** Skeletal Muscles |
| **7.** Cardiac Muscle | **8.** Striated |
| **9.** Muscle Contraction | **10.** Tendon |

**A** the muscles you can't control such as your heart

**B** the muscles that you can control

**C** a fancy word that means striped

**D** voluntary muscles that are attached to your bones and create movement

**E** made up of all of our muscles together and is responsible for the movement of the human body

**F** a tough band of tissue that connects muscles to bones

**G** an organ made up of cells called fiber tissue that can relax and contract to allow movement

**H** involuntary muscle found only in the heart

**I** when a muscle becomes thicker and shorter

**J** involuntary muscles that control the organs within your body. For Example:, they can tighten up and relax to allow food to travel through the body

# The Circulatory System

DID YOU KNOW?

The body of an adult contains over 60,000 miles of blood vessels!

# The Wonders of the Circulatory System

The main function of the circulatory system is to deliver oxygen and nutrients to all parts of the body and remove waste. The circulatory system consists of the heart, blood, and blood vessels. Your heart is a pump made of muscle about the size of your fist. It is a very important organ of the circulatory system. Your heart pumps blood through your blood vessels that carry the blood all around your body. The heart pumps about five quarts of blood every minute.

The heart has four chambers. The upper two heart chambers are called atria. It is called atrium if you are talking about only one. A wall of muscle, called the septum, separates the left atrium from the right atrium. The lower two chambers of the heart are called ventricles. Atria receive blood entering the heart. Then, the blood is sent down to the ventricles to pump blood out of the heart.

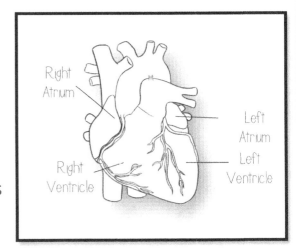

Blood flows through blood vessels. There are three types of blood vessels: arteries, veins, and capillaries. Arteries carry blood away from the heart. Veins carry blood back to the heart. Capillaries are very thin vessels that connect the arteries and veins. Their thin walls allow oxygen and nutrients to pass to and from cells.

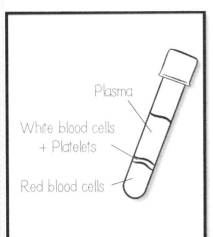

Blood is needed to keep us alive! Blood is made up of plasma, red blood cells, white blood cells, and platelets. More than half of blood is plasma. Plasma is a yellowish fluid that has nutrients, proteins, hormones, and waste products. Red blood cells deliver oxygen to cells around the body. White blood cells fight off germs such as bacteria and viruses. Your white blood cells are what protects you from having an infection. Someone with an infection will have a more than usual white blood cell count because the body will try to fight off the infection. Platelets fix veins and arteries when you have a cut. They keep the blood inside your body where it is supposed to be.

Fun fact: It only takes about 20 seconds for blood to travel through the entire circulatory system!

# The Wonders of the Circulatory System

After reading the passage, answer the questions below.

1. Which of the following is <u>not</u> a function of the circulatory system?

    a) delivers oxygen to all parts of the body
    b) breaks down food into small molecules
    c) transports nutrients to all parts of the body
    d) removes waste

2. The circulatory is made up of the _____,

    _____, and _____.

3. What are the upper two heart chambers called?

    _____

4. What are the lower two heart chambers called?

    _____

5. The _____ pump blood out of the heart.

6. Where do blood flow?

    a) through blood vessels
    b) through bones
    c) through heart muscles
    d) through the septum

7. What are the three types of blood vessels?

    _____

    _____

8. What carries blood away from the heart?

    _____

9. What carries blood back to the heart?

    _____

# The Wonders of the Circulatory System

After reading the passage, answer the questions below.

10. Which of the following connects the arteries and veins?

      a) ventricles
      b) atrium
      c) capillaries
      d) platelets

11. What is blood made up of?

   _____

   _____

12. More than half of blood is:

      a) white blood cells
      b) red blood cells
      c) platelets
      d) plasma

13. What delivers oxygen to cells around the body?

   _____

14. If you have a cut, what will fix your blood vessels to keep the blood inside your body?

   _____

15. What fights of germs such as bacteria and viruses?

   _____

16. True or false: If you have an infection, you will have a less than usual white blood cell count.

      a) True
      b) False

# Circulatory System
## Vocabulary

**Heart:** an organ that pumps blood through the body

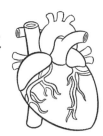

**Pulse:** a rhythmic beat felt in an artery and it is an indicator that the heart is pumping blood

**Veins:** carries blood back to the heart

**Aorta:** the largest artery in the body that carries oxygen-rich blood from the ventricle of the heart to other parts of the body

**Arteries:** carries blood away from the heart

**Platelets:** tiny cells that help your blood clot, which means that when you get a cut, your platelets will come together to help seal off the leak

**Red Blood Cells:** cells in the blood which transport oxygen to the body tissues

**Plasma:** the yellowish liquid portion of blood that has nutrients, proteins, hormones, and waste products

**White Blood Cells:** they are a key part of the immune system that fight viruses, bacteria, and other foreign invaders that threaten your health

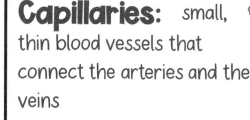

**Capillaries:** small, thin blood vessels that connect the arteries and the veins

# The Circulatory System

Use the word bank to label the circulatory system.

## Word Bank

| Heart |
|---|
| Blood Vessels |

### Answer the following questions:

1. Arteries carry blood
   a) away from the heart
   b) back to the heart

2. Veins carry blood
   a) away from the heart
   b) back to the heart

3. What are the three main types of blood vessels?

4. The main organ of the circulatory system is the

5. What is the smallest type of vessel?

# VOCAB MATCH

Find the definition for each word. Write the correct letter under each word.

| | |
|---|---|
| **1.** Heart | **2.** Veins |
| **3.** Arteries | **4.** Red Blood Cells |
| **5.** White Blood Cells | **6.** Pulse |
| **7.** Aorta | **8.** Platelets |
| **9.** Plasma | **10.** Capillaries |

**A** carries blood away from the heart

**B** small, thin blood vessels that connect the arteries and the veins

**C** the largest artery in the body that carries oxygen-rich blood from the ventricle of the heart to other parts of the body

**D** an organ that pumps blood through the body

**E** they are a key part of the immune system that fight viruses, bacteria, and other foreign invaders that threaten your health

**F** the yellowish liquid portion of blood that has nutrients, proteins, hormones, and waste products

**G** carries blood back to the heart

**H** tiny cells that help your blood clot, which means that when you get a cut, your platelets will come together to help seal off the leak

**I** cells in the blood which transport oxygen to the body tissues

**J** a rhythmic beat felt in an artery and it is an indicator that the heart is pumping blood

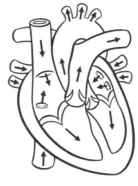

# Name the Body Systems

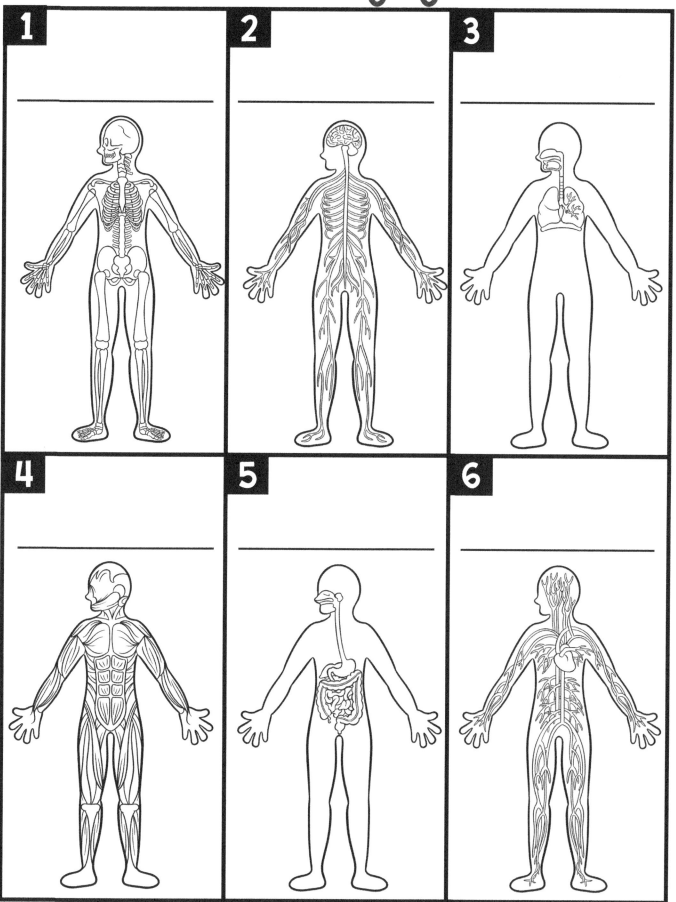

**1** _____

**2** _____

**3** _____

**4** _____

**5** _____

**6** _____

# Organ Systems – Fill in the Chart!

| System | The Organs | Function |
|---|---|---|
| Nervous System | Example: <br> • Brain <br> • Spinal Cord <br> • Nerves | Example: <br> Controls thoughts, movements, and sensory information |
| Skeletal System | | |
| Digestive System | | |
| Circulatory System | | |
| Respiratory System | | |
| Muscular System | | |

# All About

# Blood Types

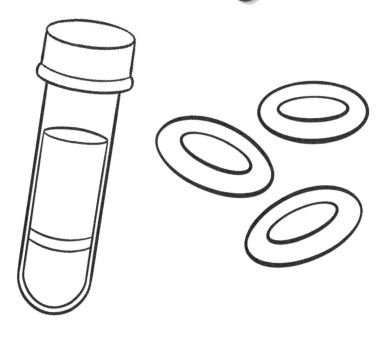

# What are Blood Types?

Did you know that not everybody has the same type of blood? Humans are very similar to one another, but when it comes to blood, there are different types. Eight to be exact! Blood types are identified as the letters A, B, and O, and are either positive or negative. The eight blood types are A+, A-, B+, B-, AB+, AB-, O+, and O-.

Red blood cells have special traits that determine the blood type. These special traits are called **antigens**. Blood can have two types of antigens: 'A antigens', and 'B antigens'. If your blood only has 'A antigens', then you are classified as type A. If your blood only has 'B antigens', then you are classified as type B. If your blood has both A and B antigens, then you are classified as type AB. If your blood has neither A nor B antigens, then you are classified as type O.

Besides the letters, a person's blood is either positive or negative. If your blood is positive, your blood has a protein called **Rh protein**. If your blood is negative, your blood does not have this protein.

It is important to know what your blood type is in case you ever lose a lot of blood during surgery, or if you want to be a donor and give blood to someone else. If you lose a lot of blood, you will need to get blood from someone else to replace the blood you lost. This transfer of blood from one person to another is called a **blood transfusion**. To get a blood transfusion, the patient must be a match with the donor. You can not take blood from just anyone without knowing if their blood type is a match. If the patient gets the wrong blood type, a serious reaction will occur. Reactions can include fever, chills, low blood pressure, and even cause kidneys to fail.

Matching blood types does not necessarily mean having the same exact blood type. For example, a person with an A+ blood type can receive blood from a person with A+, A-, O+, or O-. On the other hand, a person with an O- blood type can only receive blood from O- only, but they can give blood to all blood types. O- is the only blood type that can give blood to all blood types!

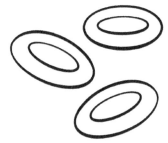

# What are Blood Types?

After reading the passage, answer the questions below.

1. How many different blood types are there?

   _____

2. What are the special traits that determine your blood type called?

   _____

3. What is the blood type of a person that has 'A antigens' in their red blood cells?

   _____

   How about if the person has 'AB antigens'? _____

   How about if the person has neither A nor B antigens? _____

4. If your blood is positive, your blood has a protein called

   _____

5. Why is it important to know what your blood type is?

   _____

   _____

   _____

   _____

6. What is a blood transfusion?

   _____

   _____

7. What can happen to a patient that receives the wrong blood type?

   _____

   _____

   _____

# Blood Type Chart

| If your blood type is: | You can give to: | You can receive from: |
|---|---|---|
| A+ | A+, AB+ | A+, A-, O+, O- |
| A- | A-, A+, AB-, AB+ | A-, O- |
| B+ | B+, AB+ | B+, B-, O+, O- |
| B- | B-, B+, AB-, AB+ | B-, O- |
| O+ | O+, A+, B+, AB+ | O+, O- |
| O- | All blood types | O- only |
| AB+ | AB+ only | All blood types |
| AB- | AB-, AB+ | AB-, A-, B-, O- |

# Donating and Receiving Blood
## Reading the blood type chart

1. Jad is a donor and wants to give blood to his relative Juliana. Jad is a B– and Juliana is a B+. Can Jad donate blood to Juliana?

2. Maria is a patient that lost a lot of blood during surgery. Maria is an O+. What blood types can Maria receive?

3. If Amir wants to donate blood, and he is AB+, what blood types can Amir donate to?

4. Sylvia needs blood. Her sister Leila wants to donate blood, but Leila does not know if Sylvia can receive her blood type. Sylvia is an A– and her Leila is a B–. Can Leila donate blood to Sylvia?

5. Adam needs blood. He is an AB+. What blood types can he receive?

6. True or False: If your blood type is O–, you can give blood to all blood types.

7. True or False: If your blood type is A+, you can receive blood from B+.

# The Heart

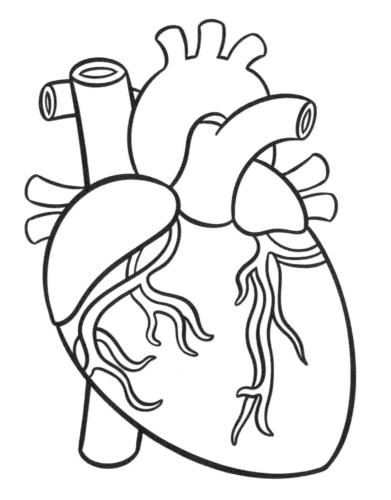

# The Human Heart

Superior Vena Cava

Aorta

Pulmonary Artery

Pulmonary Veins

Right atrium

Left atrium

Inferior Vena Cava

Right Ventricle

Left Ventricle

- o  The left and right **ventricles** pump blood out of the heart.
- o  The left and right **atria** receive blood entering the heart.
- o  The **aorta** is the main artery of the body that supplies blood to all parts of the body.
- o  The **pulmonary Artery** carries blood from the heart to the lungs.
- o  The **pulmonary Veins** carries blood from the lungs to the heart.
- o  The **superior vena cava** collects blood from your arms and head and delivers it to the heart.
- o  The **inferior vena cava** is the largest vein in the human body. It carries blood from the middle and lower body to the right atrium.

# Match and Color

Match each word on the left half of the heart puzzle piece with its definition on the right half by coloring them with the same color. The color to use for each word is indicated beneath it.

# Heart Rate Activity

How to check your pulse: Hold your hand in front of you. Place the first two fingers of your other hand inside of your wrist, below your thumb. When you have found a steady beat, count how many beats in 30 seconds (use a watch or timer) and times your score by 2. That will tell you your heart rate per minute.

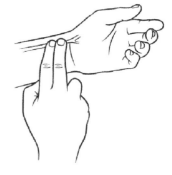

Perform each activity for <u>one minute</u>. After each activity, take your heart rate.

| Activity | Beats in 30 Seconds | Multiply x2 | Heart Rate per minute |
|---|---|---|---|
| Sit / Rest | | x2 | |
| Walk in Place | | x2 | |
| Jumping Jacks | | x2 | |
| Read a book | | x2 | |
| Stretch | | x2 | |

1. Which activity made your heart beat the fastest?


2. Which activity made your heart beat the slowest?

# Answer keys

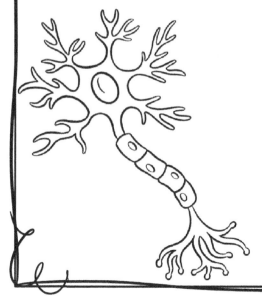

# ANSWER KEYS

## Respiratory System

### Page 9

1. C)
2. The respiratory system's main job is to bring oxygen into our bodies and send carbon dioxide out.
3. Your bloodstream
4. Carbon dioxide
5. To leave room for your heart
6. Your rib cage
7. Your diaphragm
8. Your vocal cords
9. Your protecting your body from harmful substances
10. Yawn

### Page 11

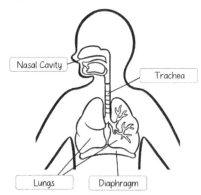

### Page 12

1. F
2. B
3. I
4. E
5. D
6. J
7. G
8. A
9. H
10. C

## Digestive System

### Page 15

1. B)
2. Food provides your body with energy, vitamins, and minerals
3. When you eat, your teeth chew the food and breaks them down into smaller pieces
4. Your saliva moistens the food and make it easier to swallow. Your saliva is also filles with chemicals and enzymes that help break down the food.
5. 4 hours
6. Your stomach release juices and acid that break down food and kills a lot of harmful bacteria so that you won't get sick.
7. False
8. Small intestine, blood
9. Any food that the body does not need or can't use is sent to the large intestine and then later leaves the body as waste.

### Page 17

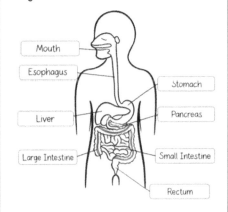

### Page 18

1. C
2. H
3. D
4. G
5. A
6. F
7. I
8. B
9. J
10. E

## Nervous System

### Page 21

1. C)
2. Brain, spinal cord, and all the nerves of your body
3. All the body's functions
4. Your nerves
5. Spinal cord
6. Brain and spinal cord
7. Nerves
8. Skull
9. Vertebrae

### Page 23

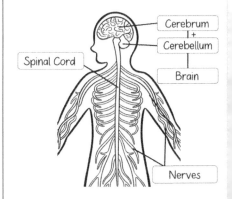

### Page 24

1. H
2. D
3. J
4. G
5. E
6. A
7. F
8. C
9. I
10. B

# ANSWER KEYS

## Skeletal System

### Page 27
1. C)
2. Bones, tendons, ligaments, cartilage
3. 206
4. Compact bone, spongy bone, bone marrow
5. Compact bone
6. B)
7. Yellow and red
8. Joints

### Page 28
9. b)
10. Elbow
11. Twisting, rotating
12. C)
13. A)
14. Tendons

### Page 30
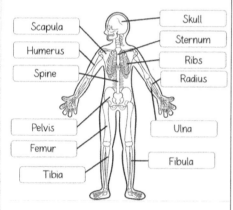

### Page 31
1. E
2. G
3. H
4. B
5. C
6. I
7. F
8. A
9. J
10. D

## Muscular System

### Page 35
1. D)
2. Over 600 muscles
3. Voluntary muscles, involuntary muscles
4. B)
5. Smooth muscles
6. You can't control your heart and make it contract and relax, therefore, it is considered involuntary..
7. Skeletal muscle

### Page 37
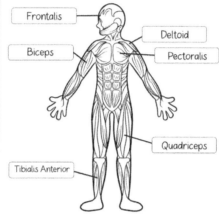

### Page 38
1. E
2. G
3. B
4. A
5. J
6. D
7. H
8. C
9. I
10. F

## Circulatory System

### Page 41
1. B)
2. Heart, blood, blood vessels
3. Atria
4. Ventricles
5. Ventricles
6. A)
7. Arteries, veins, and capillaries
8. Arteries
9. Veins

### Page 42
10. c)
11. Plasma, red blood cells, white blood cells, and platelets
12. D)
13. Red blood cells
14. Platelets
15. White blood cells
16. B)

### Page 44

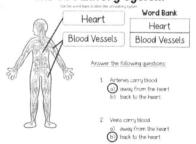

**The Circulatory System**

**Word Bank**
Heart
Blood Vessels

Answer the following questions:

1. Arteries carry blood
   a) away from the heart
   b) back to the heart

2. Veins carry blood
   a) away from the heart
   b) back to the heart

3. What are the three main types of blood vessels?
   Arteries, veins, and capillaries

4. The main organ of the circulatory system is the
   The heart

5. What is the smallest type of vessel?
   Capillaries

### Page 45
1. D
2. G
3. A
4. I
5. E
6. J
7. C
8. H
9. F
10. B

# ANSWER KEYS

## All Body Systems

### Page 47

**Name the Body Systems**

| 1 Skeletal | 2 Nervous | 3 Respiratory |
|---|---|---|
| 4 Muscular | 5 Digestive | 6 Circulatory |

### Page 48

**Organ Systems – Fill in the Chart!**

| System | The Organs | Function |
|---|---|---|
| Nervous System | Example:<br>• Brain<br>• Spinal Cord<br>• Nerves | Example:<br>Controls thoughts, movements, and sensory information |
| Skeletal System | • Bones<br>• Joints | Provides structural support, protection for internal organs, facilitates movement |
| Digestive System | • Stomach<br>• Liver<br>• Pancreas<br>• Small intestine<br>• Large intestine | Breaks down and absorbs nutrients from ingested food, eliminates waste, and supports nutrient distribution throughout the body. |
| Circulatory System | • Heart<br>• Blood vessels (arteries, veins, capillaries)<br>• Blood | Circulates blood throughout the body, transporting oxygen, nutrients, hormones, and waste products |
| Respiratory System | • Lungs<br>• Trachea<br>• Diaphragm | allows you to breathe- brings oxygen into our bodies and send carbon dioxide, a waste gas, out |
| Muscular System | • Muscles (skeletal, smooth, cardiac) | Helps your body move, generates heat, protects your internal organs, helps with food digestion |

## Blood Types

### Page 51

1. Eight
2. Antigens
3. Type A,  type AB,  Type O
4. Rh protein
5. It is important to know what your blood type is in case you ever lose a lot of blood during surgery, or if you want to be a donor and give blood to someone else.
6. The transfer of blood from one person to another
7. Serious reactions will occur, such as fever, chills, low blood pressure, and cause kidneys to fail.

### Page 53

1. Yes
2. O+ and O-
3. AB+ only
4. No
5. All blood types
6. True
7. False

## The Heart

### Page 57

NOTE: This page will be colored and you can check to see if you have the correct colors by looking at the written colors below.

- Atria — Red
- Heart — Purple
- Capillaries — Yellow
- Veins — Green
- Arteries — Orange
- Ventricles — Pink
- lower chambers of the heart — PINK
- blood vessels that carry blood away from the heart — ORANGE
- blood vessels that carry blood back to the heart — GREEN
- organ that pumps blood throughout the body — PURPLE
- upper chambers of the heart — RED
- the smallest blood vessels that connect the arteries and veins — YELLOW

Contact the author:
Fatema@thediscoveryapple.com

## Other workbooks you might like:

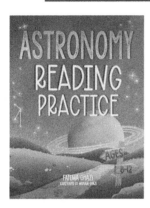

# Want Access to my FREE Resource Library?

## All in one Place!

Made in the USA
Las Vegas, NV
12 March 2024